Caught
by the Sea

ROSEMARY KEATING

illustrated by Rick Youmans

Learning Media

CONTENTS

1.
RED ROCKS

It was a calm Saturday morning. My buddy and I had decided to go diving at Red Rocks. I had never dived there before, but it was one of his favorite spots. The water can be really clear, and there's always plenty to see.

When we got to the beach, we put on our suits and checked our gear. Everything was OK, so we waded in and dived under. We had forty-five minutes of air in our tanks – enough for a good look around.

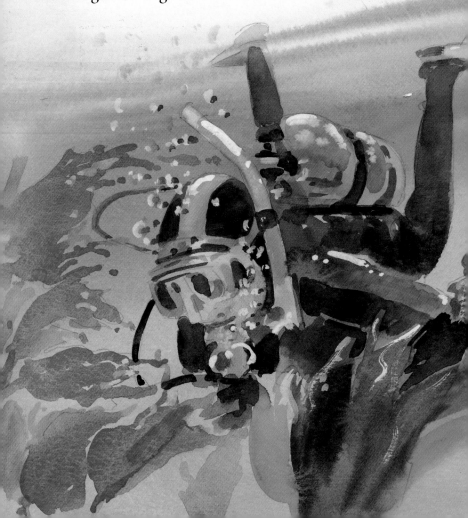

Deep down among the rocks and weeds, it was dim and quiet. It was like another world. I swam about, searching for fish or anything else that looked interesting. But I made sure that I stayed close to my buddy. That's really important when you're diving.

Suddenly I felt the water swirling around me. It picked me up and pulled me back to the surface. I didn't know what had happened, but the waves were bigger up there now. The weather was changing.

I dived down again to find my buddy, but I couldn't see him. In the dim water, I didn't even know where to start looking, so I swam back up to the surface. I could see that I was already a long way from the shore. The waves were getting stronger. They were sweeping me out to sea - and I couldn't fight them.

I blew up the part of my diving gear that works like a lifejacket. That helped me to float. I just sat there in the water, hoping that someone would come to look for me soon. Sometimes I held up my arms for help, but I couldn't keep them up for long.

Suddenly I heard the noise of an engine. I looked around and saw a little red fishing boat. It was so close – about thirty feet away. I could see three men on the boat. "Help!" I shouted. "Help me!" But the boat just went past. The waves were so high that the men hadn't seen me. That was when I started to feel frightened.

2.
I HAVE TO STAY AWAKE!

Soon I was a long way from the shore. The waves were even bigger.

They kept lifting me up and dropping me down, like a cork bobbing about on the sea. Sometimes a big wave crashed right over my head. I tried to watch for the big ones and hold my breath.

Then I saw something in the sky – a helicopter! It was flying about over by Red Rocks. My buddy must have told them that I was missing. Now the helicopter was looking for me. I waved ... and waved ... and waved! My arms got tired, and I forgot about the rough sea. I didn't see the big one coming. It crashed over me and pushed me under. When I came up, gasping for air, the helicopter had gone.

I kept looking. Maybe the helicopter would come back. Maybe it would look further out from the shore. But it didn't. In the distance, I could see a ferryboat. It was far away, but I had an idea. I got my diving knife out and held it up as high as I could. I thought someone on the ferryboat might see the knife flashing in the sun. But the boat sailed slowly away.

How long had I been in the water? Four
hours? Five? I was cold, even in my wet suit,
and I knew that was dangerous. If I got too
cold, I'd get very weak, and I wouldn't be able
to think properly.

I had to stay awake. I kept testing myself.
"What was the name of that tall girl I knew
at school? Was it Kate? Or Jane?" Then I
remembered. It was Joanna! I was still OK.

Later in the afternoon, I thought I saw another helicopter, but it was over the land – just a little dot. I didn't even wave.

3.
SUNSET

The sun was going down. It was beautiful, all gold and orange. I thought, "No one will find me now, and it'll be dark soon. If I don't do something, I'm going to die!"

So I started kicking – trying to kick myself back to the shore. But it was hard. My legs were too far down in the water. My heavy diving gear was pulling me down. I turned over onto my back. It was easier to kick like that, but I couldn't see where I was going.

Then I started thinking about sharks – I was really scared of them. Would they see my legs moving? What could I do if one swam right up to me? Once I thought I saw a fin in the dark water, but it was just a little wave.

For a long time, I knew I wasn't getting anywhere. Then ...

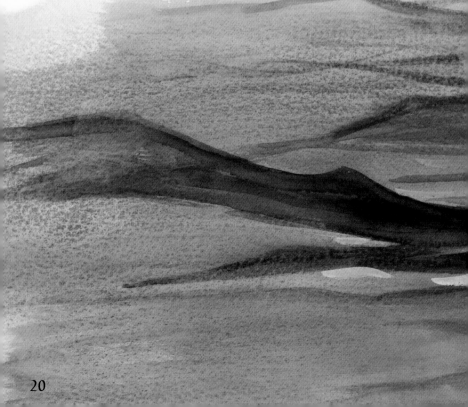

The wind felt stronger. Had it changed? Yes! It was blowing right at me. It was coming from the south. Suddenly I didn't have to kick so hard. The water started to carry me the way I wanted to go - back to the shore!

The wind was cold in my face. I had to turn over and kick on my front. When I got too tired, I had a rest on my back. On and on I went ... kicking, resting ... kicking, resting .... The night seemed to be going on forever, but I could see the lights on the shore getting closer and closer.

A seagull swooped down, close to my head. It seemed strange that it was flying in the dark. I was scared it was going to attack me, but it flew off into the night.

Then daylight came. It was wonderful! I could see that I was coming into a big bay. I kept on, kicking and kicking – watching the beach get closer. Then, at last, I was in the surf. The waves were crashing all around me. For a moment, I thought they were going to drag me under again. Then a big wave threw me up onto the beach.

4.
DRY LAND

I crawled up the sand before the sea could pull me back. I felt so heavy. My hands were swollen, but I took some of my gear off and dragged it up away from the waves. I looked back at the sea and felt so happy to be on dry land again.

It was early on Sunday morning, so the road was quiet. I couldn't see any cars at all. I didn't want to go into a house and wake someone up, so I walked along the road until I found a telephone.

I dialed the operator and said, "This is an emergency! I haven't got any money to make a call, but I need help!" I told her what had happened, and then she put the call through to my friend, Kathleen. When she answered the phone, I said, "Hi! How are you?"

"What? Who's that?" she asked.

"It's me – Rose!" I said.

"Oh, Rose," she said, "I've been crying all night! Everyone thinks you've drowned. It's been awful. Your family has called your brothers in England, and they've bought plane tickets to come home."

My friend said not to move. She'd come right away and get me. So I sat down on the side of the road and waited. Suddenly I was shivering. I thought I was going to cry. When I was out at sea, I knew that my family and friends would be worried about me. But now that I was safe, I realized - they'd thought that they would never see me again. It must have been terrible for them. I felt as if I'd come back from the dead.

My friend arrived, followed by a police car, and they took me to the nearest hospital. I was feeling OK, but I stayed there for the day so that the doctors could check me over. I had a few bruises on my face, and I was very cold and tired. But that was all that was wrong with me. Trying hard not to panic in the water, or swim against the tide, was the best thing I did. It helped me conserve my energy and keep warm enough to stay alive.

I haven't been diving since the day I was caught by the sea. I'm not too scared or worried about it. I've just had too many other things to do. I will go out diving again - one day, when my life is not so busy.